LIFE CYCLES
Frogs

by Melanie Mitchell

Lerner Publications · Minneapolis

Look at the frog.

There are many kinds
of frogs.

A frog is an **amphibian**, like a toad or a **newt**.

How does a frog grow?

A frog starts as an egg.

Frog eggs **float** in water.

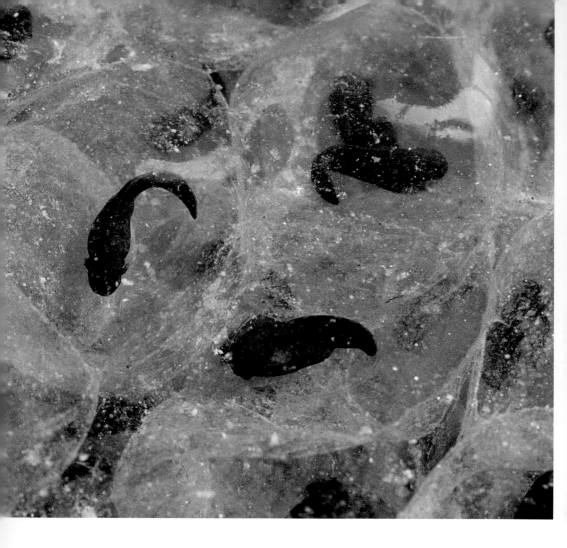

A **tadpole** grows in the egg.

The tadpole **hatches**.

At first, the tadpole looks
like a fish.

It swims like a fish, too.

The tadpole eats plants.

Later, the tadpole
grows legs.

The tadpole keeps growing
bigger.

Now it is a frog.

The young frog hops to a
new home.

It is fun to watch a
frog grow.

Parts of a Frog

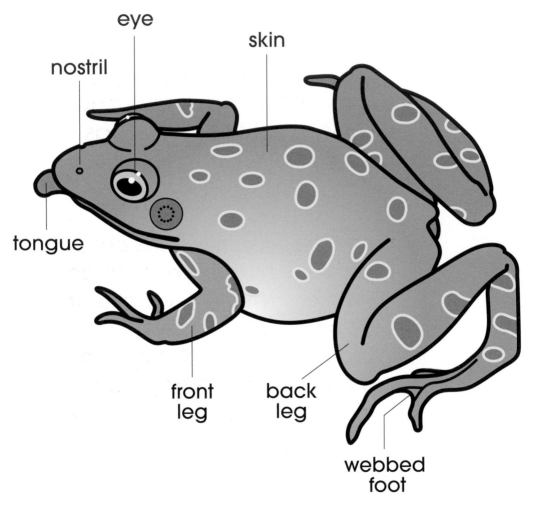

eye

skin

nostril

tongue

front
leg

back
leg

webbed
foot

Adult Frogs

Adult frogs have many body parts. Frogs have four legs. They use their back legs and webbed feet to swim. Frogs use their sticky tongues to catch insects.

When the weather turns cold, most frogs hibernate, or sleep, all winter. When they wake up, they eat a lot. Frogs eat insects, worms, and slugs. In the spring, female frogs lay their eggs, and a new frog life cycle begins.

Frog Fun Facts

 Frogs are cold-blooded. This means their body temperature adapts to their surroundings.

 Frogs swallow their food whole. Their eyeballs roll back into their head and push down on the roof of their mouth. This helps them swallow.

 Frogs won't eat dead insects.

 Frogs drink and breathe through their skin.

A group of frogs is called an army.

 In some countries, eating frog legs is considered to be a treat.

 The African Giant Frog is the largest known frog. It can grow up to 26 inches long and weigh up to 10 pounds.

 Some frogs may be hypnotized by placing them on their back and gently stroking their stomach.

Glossary

 amphibian – an animal that lives in water when young and on land when older

 float – to be held up in water or air

 hatches – comes out of an egg

 newt – a small animal that lives near water

 tadpole – a baby frog that lives in water and has a tail

Index

The photographs in this book are reproduced through the courtesy of: © William J.
Weber/Visuals Unlimited, front cover; © State of Minnesota, Department of Natural
Resources,
p. 2; © Patricia Armstrong/Visuals Unlimited, p. 3 (top right); © A. B. Sheldon, p. 3 (bottom left); © Corbis Royalty Free Images, p. 3 (top left, bottom right); © Dan Suzio, pp. 4,
6, 7, 8, 9, 10, 12, 13, 14, 15, 22 (all); © Diane Meyer, p. 5; © Ed Reschke, p. 11; ©
Stephen Dalton/Photo Researchers, p. 16; © Mary Ann McDonald/Visuals Unlimited, p.
17.
Illustration on p. 18 by Laura Westlund.

Lerner Publications Company
A division of Lerner Publishing Group, Inc.
241 First Avenue North
Minneapolis, MN 55401 USA

For reading levels and more information, look up this title at www.lernerbooks.com.

Library of Congress Cataloging-in-Publication Data

Mitchell, Melanie S.
      Frogs / by Melanie S. Mitchell.
         p.   cm. — (First step nonfiction) (Life cycles)
      Summary: A basic overview of the life cycle of a frog.
      ISBN-13: 978–0–8225–4600–9 (lib. bdg. : alk. paper)
      ISBN-10: 0–8225–4600–0 (lib. bdg. : alk. paper)
      1. Frogs—Life cycles—Juvenile literature. [1. Frogs. 2. Tadpoles.] I. Title. II.
   Series.
   QL668.E2 M58 2003
   597.8'9—dc21   2002003282

Manufactured in the United States of America
9-47350-4643-3/1/2019